Emotional Intelligence Practical Guide 2.0

Boost Your EQ and Social Skills and Learn How to Read Emotions, Analyze People, Think Like an Empath, Use Manipulation, and Persuasion for Success

Written by Travis Porter

© **Copyright 2019 Travis Porter - All rights reserved.**

The content contained within this book may not be reproduced, duplicated or transmitted without direct written permission from the author or the publisher.

Under no circumstances will any blame or legal responsibility be held against the publisher, or author, for any damages, reparation, or monetary loss due to the information contained within this book. Either directly or indirectly.

Legal Notice:

This book is copyright protected. This book is only for personal use. You cannot amend, distribute, sell, use, quote or paraphrase any part, or the content within this book, without the consent of the author or publisher.

Disclaimer Notice:

Please note the information contained within this document is for educational and entertainment purposes only. All effort has been executed to present accurate, up to date, and reliable, complete information. No warranties of any kind are declared or implied. Readers acknowledge that the author is not engaging in the rendering of legal, financial, medical or professional advice. The content within this book has been derived from various sources. Please consult a licensed professional before attempting any techniques outlined in this book.

By reading this document, the reader agrees that under no circumstances is the author responsible for any losses, direct or indirect, which are incurred as a result of the use of information contained within this document, including, but not limited to, — errors, omissions, or inaccuracies.

Table of Contents

Introduction..5

Chapter 1: What is Emotional Intelligence..........7

Chapter 2: Boost Your EQ..................................34

Chapter 3: EQ and Social Skills.........................51

Chapter 4: How to Control Your Own Emotions..62

Chapter 5: Learn How to Read Emotions..........81

Chapter 6: Learn How to Analyze People.........101

Chapter 7: Think Like an Empath....................117

Chapter 8: Use Manipulation and Persuasion for Success and Mastery..141

Conclusion..167

Introduction

Congratulations on downloading *Emotional Intelligence Practical Guide 2.0*, and thank you for doing so.

The following chapters will discuss the steps that you should take to increase your own emotional intelligence (EQ). While traditional data had assumed that IQ and mental smartness were the biggest indicators of success, recent studies have shown that emotional intelligence is the best indicator of whether someone is going to be successful or not. This guidebook will delve into some of the specifics about emotional intelligence and why it is so important.

After exploring the importance of emotional intelligence and how it can benefit your life, this guidebook will take a look at some of the steps that you can take to increase your own emotional intelligence. We will look at simple steps for boosting your EQ, how to increase your social skills, the importance of controlling your emotions, how to read emotions and analyze those of the people around you, and how you can start to think like an empath. All of these come together to help you interact better with others and see more success in your daily life.

Emotional intelligence is one of the leading determinants of whether you will be successful in your personal or professional life. This guidebook has the tools and tips that you need to make this happen!

There are plenty of other books about this subject on the market; thanks again for choosing this one! Every effort was made to ensure it is full of as much useful information as possible. Please enjoy!

Chapter 1: What is Emotional Intelligence

In many situations, emotional intelligence will be more important than your mental intelligence. While it may be impressive to have a high IQ if you want to attain success in your career and in your personal life, then having a high level of emotional intelligence is a must. You need to be able to read the signals that other people send to you and react to them accordingly. Just because you have a lot of mental smarts doesn't mean you are able to recognize and respond to the emotional cues that people give off, and this can make all the difference in your professional and personal life.

Let's say that you work in sales. Your company has a new car that has a ton of great features, and you just know the customers will love it. If you had a high level of mental intelligence, you might memorize all of the facts and features of the car, and you could spend an hour listing these off to a potential customer—but that doesn't mean you would actually be able to sell the car.

Someone with a high level of mental intelligence may be confused as to why they weren't able to sell that vehicle. They were able to get through their whole spiel about how great the car was—why wouldn't someone want to make the purchase?

On the other hand, a person with a high level of emotional intelligence might have been better at catching the signs of why someone didn't want that car. Surely there are a lot of features to love about the car—but maybe the customer was turned off by the price, wanted a van instead of a car for their growing family, or didn't like the pushy manner that was used to entice them. At some point in the conversation, the customer could have started to send out signals, sometimes spoken and sometimes not, about their disinterest in the product. With a sufficient level of emotional intelligence, you will catch these signals, and either take a step back, try recommending a different product, or find a way to address the issue and provide a better experience for your customer.

This is just one example of using emotional intelligence. Almost every career can utilize emotional intelligence to help you get ahead, but you can also use this in your personal life. Being able to read the emotions and the signals that are sent out by those around you—including your spouse, kids, friends, and other family members—can help you avoid miscommunications, hurt feelings, and so much more.

Because of all these, it is important that everyone learns how to develop mature emotional intelligence skills. These are skills that you can learn to better negotiate, empathize, and understand other people. This is even truer in a world that is becoming more globally connected.

Your EQ, or your emotional intelligence, is the ability you have to understand other people. It is your ability to understand what motivates other people and your ability to work cooperatively with them. Without this, it can be really hard to get along with different people, no matter how you interact with them.

The Five Categories Involved in Emotional Intelligence

When we look at the different aspects of emotional intelligence, it is important to realize that there are actually five different categories that come with it. These include self-awareness, self-regulation, motivation, empathy, and social skills. It is possible to have a higher score in one or two of these but still struggle with the others. Some people do well in all areas besides one. No matter which area is lacking for you, it is possible to build up your emotional intelligence and use it as a way to get along with those around you better. Let's take a look at each of these categories to learn more about why they matter to your emotional intelligence.

Self-awareness

The first category is self-awareness. When working with emotional intelligence, the ability to recognize emotions as they are happening is very important. This can be hard for some people to do because it will require you to have the ability to tune into your own true feelings. If you are able to evaluate your own emotions, you will be more capable to manage them.

There are many different parts that come with self-awareness. You need to understand what feelings you have at a certain time. You need to understand why you are feeling a specific emotion. And you need to look at these emotions and figure out if they are actually justified emotions or ones that you fit with the situation at hand. Some of the major elements that come with self-awareness include:

- Emotional awareness: With emotional awareness, you have the ability to recognize your own emotions, how they can affect your mood, and how you behave and react to others.
- Self-confidence: This refers to the certainty that you have about your own capabilities. If you don't have a high level of self-confidence, then it can be really hard to have good self-awareness.

Before you are able to understand the emotions that others face and use them to relate to those around you, you must first be able to understand the emotions that you are facing yourself. Building up your self-awareness is one of the best ways to do this.

Self-regulation

To increase your emotional intelligence, you must also be able to regulate yourself. Oftentimes, you will have very little control over when you will experience an emotion. Emotions have a way of hitting us, sometimes when we least expect it. You can't control when this happens, and it is important to realize that having these emotions is not a bad thing. However, the way that you react to these emotions is under your control. You can have a say in how you react to the emotions and even in how long those particular emotions will last. There are various techniques that you can rely on to help alleviate some of those negative emotions—such as depression, anxiety, and anger—that seem to just stick around.

Rather than letting these emotions take over and stick around for a long time, you can work on self-regulation to recognize that you have these emotions, validate them, and then use the right techniques to make them disappear.

When it comes to feeling these negative emotions, it is important to see that you just need to change the situation around. If the situation is making you angry or sad, think of ways to turn it around and make it more positive. There are several different things that you can do to help change the situation and put it under a more positive light. Things like meditation or a long walk with nature can make a big difference in how you feel. You can't always control when the emotion shows up—but you can always change the way that you react to that situation, and looking at it from a different view can make a difference.

To gain more self-regulation, you will need the following:

- Self-control: This is when you are able to manage some of the disruptive impulses that you feel.
- Trustworthiness: Not only must you be able to trust other people; you must also be able to trust yourself. Make sure to hold yourself to a standard of integrity and honesty from the start.
- Conscientiousness: This factor means that you take responsibility for the way that you perform, whether you did a good job or not.
- Adaptability: Things are going to happen in life, and being flexible to these changes can make it easier to enjoy life and not get so upset.
- Innovation: To have high emotional intelligence, you must keep yourself open to new ideas.

Motivation

The next category to work on with your emotional intelligence is motivation. The best way to keep yourself motivated to any achievement you receive is to have clear goals and a positive attitude. There are some people who find this easier to do because they are predisposed to a better outlook on life. There are also those who find this hard to do because they are predisposed to a more negative attitude. No matter which one describes you, it is possible to train your mind to think in a more positive manner.

Having a positive outlook on life, even when things aren't going your way, can really help you control your own emotions. It takes some effort. Over the years, most people have slowly trained their minds to be negative about everything, even if something good is going on for them.

If you are able to teach yourself to catch negative thoughts as they go through your mind, then you can take that thought and reframe it in a positive way. Over time, you will get better at doing this, and you will automatically change all thoughts to positive ones to achieve your goals.

When it comes to motivation, you will find that it is made up of the following:

- Achievement drive: You must have a high drive for achievement to help with your motivation. Your achievement drive is going to be you striving to improve or meet your own standards of excellence.
- Commitment: You must be committed to your goals to see success. To help with your commitment, make sure to align your goals with that of the organization or the group that you work with.

- Initiative: This is the process of getting yourself ready to act when an opportunity presents itself.
- Optimism: It is hard to stay motivated towards a goal if you are negative and down about the work. If you feel forced into the work or that it is a horrible idea, then your motivation will be gone soon. Optimism can make it easier to persistently pursue all your goals, no matter what setbacks and obstacles come your way.

Empathy

If you want to be successful in your personal life and in your career, then you must have the ability to recognize how those around you are feeling. Some people seem to be able to read the thoughts and emotions of those around them while others struggle with this. The more empathy you have, the easier this process can be.

The better you are at discerning the feelings behind the signals others send to you, the better off you will be. This can even help you control what signals you are sending out to others. Someone who is empathetic will excel at the following:

- Service orientation: This is when you are able to anticipate or recognize the needs of your clients and then meet these needs.
- Developing others: Part of emotional intelligence is pushing others along and encouraging them to meet their own goals. You will be able to sense what things others will need to improve, and you can be there to bolster up their abilities as well.
- Leveraging diversity: If there is diversity in your group or your company, you will be able to cultivate all the opportunities that come from this diversity.

- Political awareness: There are times you will join a new group. This group has different relationships, different people in power, and different structure. Those who have a higher emotional intelligence will be able to recognize these emotional currents and the power relationships in a new group.
- Understanding others: Those who have a lot of empathy will be able to understand and see the feelings that are behind the wants and needs of those around them.

Social skills

Emotional intelligence also requires that you have great social skills to interact with those around you. Having good interpersonal skills is so important in your career and in your personal life. In our modern world where everyone is always connected, you will find that the people around you also have instant access to technical knowledge.

While more people are hooked into technology, many of them are lacking in people skills. They can run a computer, use a smartphone, and work with a wide variety of technological items, but many don't know how to properly interact with others.

Having these people skills can be so important, as it has been quite rare nowadays. Being able to interact with and respond to the emotions and signals that someone else is sending out is a skill that many are lacking. Having it can ensure that you are able to negotiate, empathize, and even understand anyone you come in contact with. Some of the things that you will find the most useful when it comes to social skills include:

- Influence: You need to have the right persuasion tactics in place to convince others to listen to you or to react in a certain way.

- Communication: Not only should you be able to talk to anyone; you should also be able to listen. You must learn how to send out clear messages to your listeners.
- Leadership: Those with good social skills are able to inspire others and can guide them.
- Change catalyst: Social skills help you manage and initiate any changes that you think are necessary.
- Conflict management: In any career and in many situations in your personal life, conflicts are going to arise. Social skills will help you understand and resolve any disagreements that may come up.
- Building bonds: Nothing is better for building up relationships and bonds than the right social skills.
- Collaboration and cooperation: Even if you don't always see eye to eye with others in your group, good social skills can make it easier to work with other people.

- Team capabilities: Those with good social skills can work well with a group and may complement those who have different skills.
-

How Personality, IQ, and Emotional Intelligence are Different

When the idea of emotional intelligence was first introduced in 1995, it was the missing link that people were looking for. Many studies revealed that seventy percent of the time, those who had an average IQ were able to perform better than those who had the highest IQ numbers. In the business world that believed IQ was the biggest indicator of success, it first seemed impossible that those with lower IQ were the ones getting ahead career-wise.

This kind of anomaly threw a big wrench into the idea that many people had with regards to success. After decades of research related to this, it is now believed that emotional intelligence is a critical factor far more important than IQ in setting star performers apart from others in a group.

While some people are able to have high IQ and high emotional intelligence at the same time, those who only rely on their IQ are the ones who end up not being that successful. Emotional intelligence is an intangible factor that is inside of everyone. It is in control of how people manage their behavior, navigate the social rules of their world, and make personal decisions that will give them positive results.

Emotional intelligence is able to tap into some of the fundamental elements of human behavior, and these are very distinct from your mental intellect. There isn't a connection between emotional intelligence and your IQ. You aren't able to predict how emotionally intelligent someone will be based on their mental smarts. There are some who have high IQs who also have high emotional intelligence, yet there are also those who have lower IQ but have high emotional intelligence. It all depends on the individual.

Your personality is the final part of this puzzle. It is a style that is pretty stable and will define each of you. Your personality is going to be the end result of hard-wired preferences, such as your inclination to be an extrovert or an introvert.

Just like your IQ, the personality of a person isn't necessarily an indicator of your emotional intelligence. And just like your IQ, your personality will remain relatively stable throughout your lifetime and won't change much under normal circumstances. Your emotional intelligence, on the other hand, can change throughout your lifetime as long as you work on it. The emotional intelligence, IQ, and personality of a person will help in telling you more about a person and can even tell you what makes that person tick.

How Your Emotional Intelligence can be Linked to Performance

One question that comes up here is how much your emotional intelligence is going to affect your professional success. To keep it short, the emotional intelligence is going to affect your success a lot. This type of intelligence is a powerful way for you to focus your energy in one direction to get the best results.

A study was done by TalentSmart testing 33 workplace skills against emotional intelligence. The results were that emotional intelligence was one of the strongest predictors of performance. In fact, it was able to account for a whopping 58 percent of success, no matter what type of job was discussed.

Your personal emotional intelligence is an important foundation for many skills that are critical to professional success. In fact, it has the power to impact almost everything that you do during the day. Out of several studies, the top 90 percent of performers had a high emotional intelligence score. On the other side, only twenty percent of those at the bottom are high in emotional intelligence.

It is possible to be considered a top performer in your field without a lot of emotional intelligence, but the work is a lot harder to accomplish. Having this emotional intelligence can make it easier to get to the top because you know how to control your own emotions, how to react to different situations, how to be flexible, and how to read other people. As a result, those with higher emotional intelligence are often given promotions and more responsibilities at work, and on average they earn around $29,000 per year more than others in the field. These findings are true no matter what industry you are working with.

The Benefits of a High Emotional Intelligence

There are many benefits to working on your emotional intelligence. It can improve all aspects of your personal and professional life. Some of the benefits of working on your emotional intelligence include:

- Better relationships: Your emotional intelligence can directly affect the relationships that you have with your children, partners, spouses, and friends. It can even help you with your business relationships. According to a study published in *Personality and Individual Differences*, those who have a higher EQ reported that they had higher satisfaction with their personal relationships.
- Better self-control: If you are one of those people who get angry easily, snap at those around you, or experience things like road rage, then it may be time to work on your

EQ. Anger can cause a lot of damage to others and to yourself, especially when it's not controlled. Developing a good emotional intelligence can help strengthen your self-control. You can then understand those strong emotions, such as anger—so that you can manage it, direct it, and handle it appropriately.

- Greater job performance and satisfaction: According to a study found in *The Leadership Quarterly*, professionals who had higher EQ experienced higher productivity levels and more job satisfaction compared to others. In addition, according to another study found in the *Journal of Organizational Behavior,* the higher your EQ, the better your job performance.
- Less stress at work: According to a study done in *The International Journal of Organizational Analysis,* those who have higher emotional intelligence tend to

experience less stress in the workplace. Those with higher EQ scores also tended to have more commitment to their work or organization.

- Higher levels of happiness: Those who have a higher level of emotional intelligence seem to be happier. This can be because they already know what makes them happy, and they refuse to let others around them limit the personal happiness that they feel. They have the understanding that they, and only they, are in control of their emotions. This realization not only leads to a higher inner strength, but it can lead to feeling happier and a better sense of well-being. A study from *Personality and Individual Differences* showed that emotional intelligence was associated with positive life outcomes for those who had it.

You Can Develop Your Emotional Intelligence

If you read through this and feel that maybe your emotional intelligence is low, don't fret. You are not stuck in your current position. You are not stuck earning less and never getting a promotion. Emotional intelligence is a skill that you can develop, no matter where yours is at the time.

Using strategies that are there to increase your emotional intelligence can allow all the neurons in your brain to develop and change. It takes some hard work and will not be an instant change, but using the right strategies can make this happen. It may seem difficult when you first get started. Your brain is trained to react to situations in one way, and you are trying to convince it to think in a whole new way. But with some practice and some patience with yourself, you will see results. And it doesn't matter how long before you are finally able to develop your emotional intelligence; you will still be able to get all the benefits that come with it in your personal and professional life.

It doesn't matter where your emotional intelligence is at this point. You may have a low emotional intelligence and find that it is difficult to be in social situations, read the emotions of others, or even control your own emotions. Maybe you are good at reading others, but you struggle with keeping your own emotions under control. Each person is different, and everyone has some area of emotional intelligence that they need to work on.

The important thing to remember is that your emotional intelligence is something that you can improve. Don't think that you are stuck in your current EQ situation. You have the power to change it. Just follow some of the steps that we discussed in this guidebook, and over time you will see your emotional intelligence improve.

Emotional intelligence is a major factor in your life. It helps you to get along better in social situations. It can help you control some of your own emotions and how you react to situations around you. It can make such a big difference in your personal and professional life.

Chapter 2: Boost Your EQ

After learning more about the importance of your emotional intelligence, you may want to learn some of the methods that you may use to help increase your emotional intelligence or your EQ. No matter where your emotional intelligence is in the beginning, you can follow different techniques to boost your EQ and make it stronger. This chapter is going to look at the different steps you can take to boost the various categories of your EQ to get the best results.

Get Out There With Nature

The first thing that you need to do to help your emotional intelligence is to get away from all the worries and all the stress of your life, and the best way to do that is to get out with nature.

It is too easy to get caught up in our daily lives. We spend too much time on our computers and on social media, comparing our lives with the perfect pictures that others seem to have. It is easy to get caught up in work, taking home with us the demands of our jobs and barely getting a break. It is easy to just let stresses, drama, and other things get in the way of our clear thinking, and these soon take over our lives.

All this negativity, all this technology, and just all the stress from a regular life can really affect the way that we handle our emotions. It can even mess with the emotions that we have. Taking some time to get away from all this can make a difference in how well we can handle our emotions and can increase our EQ levels.

Getting out into nature can make a big difference. There is just something about being outside, being with nature and away from all the gadgets and stressors and other problems in the world. It can really clear the head and will have a meditative effect on you. Even ten minutes a day outside can make a difference. And if you can add some physical activity to your time outside—whether that is a moderate walk around the block or a sweat-inducing run, you will see the results of this time with nature in just a few minutes.

The next time that you feel that the stresses of your life are taking over, or you feel that your emotions are getting the best of you, then it is time to get outside. Half an hour can do wonders for calming your breathing, getting you to relax, and helping you regulate the emotions that you feel.

Take the Actions That Are Needed to Wake up Your Own Conscious Mind

Life isn't always as predictable as you may like. Sometimes the solutions that you are seeking won't come to you easily. There are no rules that you should follow, and it is hard work to define the path that you must take.

When you are able to wake up your conscious mind, you will be better prepared to accept your reality and embrace any change and unpredictability that come up in your life, and you can then take a step towards finding the path that will lead you to the right decisions.

Each person is going to have something that is in their way. Whether they are low on self-confidence or they are dealing with limiting self-beliefs, these things are holding them back from being true to themselves and reaching their potential. And whether they admit or recognize it at all, this can be very frustrating, leading them to less control over their emotions.

Ask for Help from Others

Even after knowing all of the benefits that come with increasing your emotional intelligence, you are still going to run into times that are difficult. You may have an emotion that gets out of hand. You may get angry or sad or feel guilty and not be able to handle it in a manner that showcases your high EQ, and this is perfectly normal. Working on your emotional intelligence is a process, one that you will work on for the rest of your life.

If you are struggling with your emotions and controlling your emotional intelligence, then maybe you should consider finding someone who can help you on this journey. Find someone you can talk to when your emotions seem to go out of control. Find someone who can provide you with advice and strategies any time you get stuck. Find someone who supports your adventure of gaining a higher EQ and who can be there any time that you need their assistance.

Get to Know Yourself Better

If you don't take the time to learn more about yourself and your emotions, you will never increase your EQ. You have to know about your emotions, why you react to things a certain way, and what some of your triggers are. Failing to do so can make it almost impossible to really understand your emotions. If you aren't able to understand your own emotions, how can you expect to understand the emotions of others?

This is hard for many people to accomplish. You may just let your emotions come out, without thinking them through. You assume that all the emotions you are feeling are natural and that they are legitimate, but has there ever been a situation where you felt angry and later found out that there really wasn't a reason to feel that way? This probably happens more in your life than you may like to admit.

Learning more about your emotions and how you personally react to situations can make all the difference. The way that you react to some situations may be different from the way others react to them. Why would this be true? This is just one of the questions that you should ask yourself when learning about yourself and your emotions.

Meditation is one of the best techniques that you can use to help with this. Meditation not only teaches you how to relax and slow down your breathing to get rid of stress, but it also presents you with a way to detach from your emotions, both negative and positive, so you can observe them. You are not there to judge your emotions. All emotions are valid, and there is a reason you are feeling them. But with mindfulness and meditation, you can take a look at those emotions, and figure out if it is one you want to feel right now, or if you would rather put your time and energy towards something else.

This process takes time. Meditation alone can be hard for those who are always worrying about something that happened in the past and the present or fretting about the future. And sometimes people get so caught up in the emotions that they experience that it seems impossible to look at them objectively. But over time, they can gain the right skills to make this happen.

Focus on Others More

Those who have a higher level of emotional intelligence will spend a lot of their time paying attention to others rather than on themselves. They are able to listen and empathize with others before anything else.

Being able to turn your attention outwards can give you a chance to notice how others are feeling. When your emotions are outwards rather than inwards, you can easily notice when a friend or a colleague is dealing with a bad day, and you can respond by listening to them. Sometimes the best thing that you can do for someone else is just giving them some of your time and attention when they are having a rough time.

When you focus more on others, you will start to develop more empathy in the process. Empathy allows you to put yourself in the shoes of someone else to make it easier to see what they're going through. It's not always enough to see things from the perspective of another person. You need to take this much deeper and figure out the whys of their experiences. Why would this person feel a certain way? What events may have led them to feel or think this way?

Another part of this is learning how to be curious about other people. Those with naturally high EQs are more interested in those around them than they are in themselves. If you are working on improving your EQ, make some effort to talk to others, especially those who may be different from you or whom you don't know well. Be polite but inquisitive, and try to see things from that person's point of view.

Work on Your Listening Skills

Most people are going to listen with the intent to reply to the other person, rather than with the intent of understanding them. But to have a high EQ, you must have some active listening skills. Instead of focusing so much on how you can reply to what the other person says, you must give that person your full attention while they speak, so you can actually understand what they are saying.

To work with your listening skills, make sure that you give them your full attention. Put your phone down, turn off anything that you might find distracting, keep your own feelings and thoughts, and don't spend much time thinking about what you will say next. Just listen to what the other person is saying.

As you listen to the other person, keep your mind open, and try to understand where that other person is coming from. Never judge them or jump to conclusions, and never interrupt what they say. Interrupting the other person implies that you think you are more important than them, and this can really damage relationships.

While you are listening, make sure to pay attention to other things besides what the person is saying. You can look at their vocal tone, their facial expressions, and their body language. These things really give out some important clues as to what the other person is feeling when they talk. And if there is ever a time when they say something that you don't understand, ask for clarification rather than jumping to assumptions.

Admit When You Make a Mistake

There will be times in your life when you make mistakes. Most will fail to admit when a mistake happens. They will blame others, hide from the mistake, and ignore that it even happened. But those who have a higher amount of emotional intelligence aren't scared to admit when a mistake is made, and if needed, they will apologize.

It is never easy to admit that a mistake occurred, especially if you are not used to it. To help you get accustomed to this, think about when you made a mistake in the past. What happened when you were in these situations? Did you end up putting the blame over to someone else, sweeping this mistake under the rug, or did you take responsibility for the situation? How did you feel when that situation was over?

No one is perfect, and it is so important to acknowledge that to yourself. Taking responsibility for your actions, whether it is for the good things that you did or your mistakes, can help build up trust and can make your integrity stronger. People respect those who are vulnerable and who are committed to making things right when mistakes are made.

Other Methods to Use to Enhance Your Emotional Intelligence

- Work to stop changing or interrupting the subject: There will be times you have feelings that are a little bit uncomfortable. No one likes to feel this way. Instead of dealing with these types of emotions, they will try to distract themselves or try to interrupt and change the emotion. Instead of doing this, choose to sit down a few times a day, and ask yourself how you are feeling. Sometimes the emotions will come flooding forward; other times it can take a bit. Allow yourself to feel your emotions, no matter what they are, for that small amount of time.

- Don't judge your feelings too quickly: It is fine to feel angry sometimes. It is fine to feel sad sometimes. It is also fine to feel disappointed, upset, happy, joyful, depressed, and all other emotions sometimes. What's important is that you learn to not dismiss your feelings before you can think them through. You will soon find that your emotions are often going to rise and then fall—rising, peaking, and fading naturally. You don't want to cut off that wave before it peaks. Doing so will mean you are pushing that emotion away, and this may result in a big explosion later on. You may not feel good about that emotion, but you still need to let it come out on occasion.

- Is there a connection between this current feeling and another time in the past: When you notice a particularly difficult feeling coming out, it is time to do some self-discovery, and see if you've had that feeling before. Doing this can help you see if your current emotional state is tied to a time in your past or to the situation you are going through right now.

- The connection between your feelings and your thoughts: There are times when an emotion will hit you that seem out of the ordinary. When this happens, it is a good idea to ask yourself what you think about this. Often, one of the feelings you are having will contradict the others, which is perfectly normal. Sometimes, listening to all those feelings can be like listening to a variety of witnesses in a court case. Only by admitting all the evidence that is at hand will you come to the best verdict.

- Listen to your body: Sometimes the hints that we need to our emotions will show themselves in physical form. For example, if you notice that you get a knot in your stomach on the way to work, it may be a sign that your job causes you stress. Listening to the physical sensations that show up can really give you insight into your emotions.

- If you aren't sure about how you are feeling, it may be time to ask someone else: It is possible to ask someone else how you are coming across. This can give you some good insight into the emotions you are feeling at the time.

- Take time to ask yourself how you are feeling: You can start out this questioning session by rating your overall sense of well-being. You can use any scale that you would like. Keep these ratings in a daily log book. If you notice that you have one day where these ratings seem pretty extreme, you can take some time to review if there are any associations or ideas that are interconnected.

- Write down your feelings and thoughts: There is a lot of research that shows how your feelings and thoughts can be improved simply by writing them down. A simple exercise like writing down your emotions on a journal can take just a few minutes each day. Nonetheless, it provides you with some amazing insight into your emotions and how you are able to handle them.
- Know when you have reached your limits: There is going to be a time, which is different for everyone, where you should stop looking inwards and shift your focus to looking outwards. Studies have shown that when you continue to dwell on your negative feelings, they will be amplified.

Emotional intelligence is not just about looking within but also about learning how to be truly present in the world around you.

Chapter 3: EQ and Social Skills

One part of your emotional intelligence is how well you are able to communicate and interact with other people. Some people are really good at getting along with others. They can walk into a room and be friends with everyone there. They are the life of the party. They know how to act no matter the situation. And they always seem to know the right thing to say.

But there are many people who are on the other side of this. These people find that they are socially awkward when they go out. No matter how much they want to, they find that it is hard to talk to people and to make new friends. They go to different settings and find that they wish they were back home.

With your emotional intelligence, you need to have a certain amount of social skills. You don't need to enjoy going out each night and being out socializing all the time, but you do need to have the right social skills in order to get along with others, as well as know how to engage people in a conversation and how to read them. This will help you in so many aspects of your life, even in your professional career.

How to Enhance Your Verbal Communication

The first thing we will concentrate on is your verbal communication. This will be the words that you say to someone else. The way that you communicate verbally will make a big difference in how people respond to you, and whether or not you will get them to like you or open up to you.

To start, you need to be aware of the tone and the volume of your voice. Be careful about speaking too softly or too loudly when you are meeting new people. Choose a volume that can be heard easily. This volume is going to change based on whether you are in a crowded and loud space versus meeting someone in the office or at home. A volume that is easy to hear suggests that you are confident but not aggressive. If you are unsure about the right volume, try to match yours with that of the people around you.

You can also watch out for the speed of your words. If you speak too quickly, not only it is hard to understand what you are saying, but it also shows that you lack confidence around others. If you are in a conversation and start speaking too fast due to nerves, then try to speak about a third of your normal speed. This is a trick that many people use, and it is called slow talk. It helps you speak in a clear fashion and also calms down those nerves a bit.

Next, you need to learn the right manner to use in order to begin a new conversation. Stick with something simple to open up the conversation. Go with something that is generally true, rather than something that is really personal because this can come off as offensive or insulting to some people. It is best to stick with options like the weather or a new story that you heard on the news recently. You can also compliment someone on what they are wearing. This helps to break the ice a little bit and helps you and the other person get more comfortable with each other.

In some cases, starting with small talk is not always an easy thing to handle. You want to say something that will get the conversation going, but you don't want to get too personal with someone you are just meeting for the first time. Knowing what to say can be hard. Some examples of ways to get started on a conversation include:

- "I love the view from here."
- "Hasn't the weather been crazy lately?"
- "That is a nice shirt. Where did you get it?"
- "Isn't that history class really interesting?"

Once you have done some small talk to get the conversation started, it is time to find ways to extend it out. This is where you can try bringing up some topics that are more relatable or more intimate. You can ask more questions here in hopes of getting below the surface a bit. For example, you can spend this time asking about the other person's hobbies, employment, or family. This opens up the floor for both of you to continue talking and can make the conversation more meaningful.

During this time, the most important thing to remember is that a conversation needs two people to work. You should avoid speaking too little or too much during that conversation. Try to ask questions that are open-ended so the other person has to elaborate a bit and can't just give yes-or-no answers. This allows them to talk further and gives you more material to react on when it is your turn to speak.

In most social situations, you will want to stay away from any topic that may be considered inflammatory. This is really important if you are around those you don't know too well. This means that topics such as ethnicity and race, politics, and religion should be kept for a different time. It is fine to ask someone a question about the election that is coming up, but some people will find that it is offensive to ask who they are going to vote for.

And finally, when the conversation is reaching its natural end, it is important that you leave the other person on a good note. It is never acceptable to abruptly cut off the other person and walk away. Instead, find a more courteous manner in order to take your leave. You want to give the other person the impression that you had a good time and enjoyed that interaction. If you are stuck on things to say when it is time to naturally end the conversation, try some of the following to make this easier:

- "I can see that you are busy, so I'll let you go. It was nice talking to you."
- "I have an appointment to get to, but it has been fun to chat with you."
- "I've got to run, but I hope we meet again soon."

How to Improve Your Nonverbal Communication

Now that you have some ideas on how to talk to the other person, it is time to work on some of your nonverbal cues. You can say all the right things to the other person, but if your nonverbal cues are wrong, then this is never going to work out for you.

The first thing here that you need to pay attention to is body language. The gestures that you use will often communicate a message that is way more powerful than the words that you use. Be wary and take some time to reflect on the messages that you end up sending out to others through your facial expressions, eye contact, and posture. Some things that you should watch out for include:

- If you cross your arms, stand far away from others, and refuse to let them get close, then you are giving off the signal that you aren't interested in interacting with them.
- Always keep your pose confident, and smile as much as you can.
- Keep eye contact with the other person. Stand tall, and keep those arms unfolded.

Sometimes it is hard to know how to behave in a social situation. The best thing to do here is to observe how other people do it. Look at their body language, and see what may show up there that lets them be better at interacting in a social way. Watch their eye contact, their facial expression, their posture, and their gestures. When you have a good idea of what they are doing and how they are successful, you can use some of those to improve how your nonverbal cues are in public.

If there is one nonverbal cue that is really important when you are meeting someone new, it is your smile. You want to show off a genuine smile from the moment you meet someone up to the moment they walk away. A smile is known all over the world as a way to show others that you are open to them, and it can do wonders for making others feel at ease around you. Focus on smiling as naturally as possible when you meet someone new, and it can make things easier for you.

You can also take time to practice your eye contact. If you are not very good at making eye contact with others, or if you find that doing this makes you feel uncomfortable, then it may be time to get some practice. You don't want to stare people right in the eyes, especially if you feel uncomfortable with doing this because it will be annoying. Start out with just looking in the eye of someone else for about three to five seconds only. Over time, this will get easier, and you will feel more natural about doing it.

If you are not standing right next to the person you are talking with, then try to look at someplace other than their eyes to get started. You can go with their earlobe or at a spot that is right between the eyes. This is technically faking it, but the person you are talking to will have no idea. You can also try making eye contact with people on TV to get some practice. Turn on the news, and while watching, try to maintain eye contact with the news anchor.

Finally, when you are getting yourself ready to go out, make sure to spend a little extra time on this. When you look good, you feel good, and the more confidence you will have. Pick outfits that make you feel good and will fit the occasion you are heading out to, and you will have the confidence you need to handle any social situation.

Travis Porter

Chapter 4: How to Control Your Own Emotions

One important aspect of emotional intelligence is the ability to control your own emotions. Many times it is easy to let the emotions take control of you. You may be able to keep those emotions under control, but you may not be able to handle them properly and end up letting them all out at the worst possible time. Here is the time to learn some of the best tips to help you control and properly manage your emotions to prevent a disaster later on.

How to Refocus Your Mind and Your Body

Here, we need to start by noticing when an emotion is getting away from you, or when it is out of control. Ask yourself what this will feel like, both to you mentally and physically, and then you can work to identify when these emotions are happening at the moment. Catching your emotions when they are first starting to go out of control but before they reach that point can require some mindfulness and rational thought. Of course, this may seem hard to do at the moment, but just recognizing the emotion when it occurs can help ground you. Some of the signs that you can look for when checking to see if an emotion is getting away from you include:

- Look for some of the physical reactions. This can include rapid breathing, tense muscles, and a faster heart rate.
- There are also mental reactions to these emotions. You may feel overwhelmed or anxious. Often you may feel that you have no control over your thoughts.
- When this happens, you need to slow down and focus on just one part of the reaction at a time—so if you feel anxious, notice what is this feeling like in your body. You may notice that your palms are

sweaty and your heart is beating fast. Acknowledge and accept these as they are, but never judge them.

Any time your emotions seem to be getting out of control, nothing will work better than some deep breathing to calm down. Before the spiral starts to catch up to you, cut it off with a few deep breaths to calm down the body and the mind. A good technique to try out is the following:

- Place one hand on your chest above the heart and the other right below your rib cage. Take a deep breath in slowly through the nose while counting to four. Feel the stomach and the lungs expand as they fill up with air.
- Hold this breath for a few counts before slowly letting that breath out of your mouth. You should only get about six to ten deep breaths in each minute.

- Keep doing this until you can feel the heart noticeably slow down, and you feel that the rapid breathing is done.

You can also choose to focus on a more physical sensation to help center your mind again. Sometimes losing control of the emotions can end up with you losing your self and your place. You can get lost in your emotions and then lose awareness of where you are. To help counter this, you may want to force yourself to notice the things that are right next to you or the physical sensations that you are going through. Some of the ways that you can concentrate on these sensations include:

- Try working on some grounding exercises. These are going to engage all the senses so that you can root into the present moment. Speaking aloud is really important because it forces the brain to move away from the emotions. Coming back into the body and then focusing on the present moment can help you to become grounded better and can stop the emotional spiral.

- Take a moment and look around the room. Talking out loud, describe the things that you see. Listen for the sounds. Notice the smells, and see if there are any tastes that you can identify. Say all of these out loud to help ground yourself.
- Take notice of what is physically touching you. Notice the coffee that is in your hands, how your clothes feel, whether you are tense or sore, and even what it feels like to sit in your chair.
- Brew some coffee and then focus intently on the sensation of drinking that. You can ask a lot of questions such as how does it taste, how does the cup feel, and what does it smell like. Make sure that you answer the questions out loud.

Visualization can be so important in this process as well. Sometimes the best way to calm your emotions and make yourself feel better is to learn how to relax the muscles to relieve tension and then visualizing yourself in a calm and safe place. The fun thing about this is that you can choose your own calming place, so it can be as unique as you want.

To come up with this calm and safe place, you need to choose a place (it doesn't matter if it is real or imagined) that you find tranquil and soothing. Any time that an emotion is sneaking up on you, close your eyes and imagine that place. In your mind, create as many details as you can about that place while taking in slow breaths. Let the tension slowly leave the body, and let the calmness of your safe place quiet all your thoughts and emotions.

Your safe place can be anywhere that you like. Some ideas include your bedroom, a temple, a spa, or a beach. It just needs to be a place where you can feel relaxed and safe. When you come up with the place, think about the sounds that are there, the things that you could see, and the textures and the smells that are present.

If there is ever a time when you are in that safe and calming space and notice that there is a negative emotion at the same time, imagine it as some kind of object that you can easily remove from the safe place. For example, if you are feeling worried or stressed, you can visualize it as a pebble that you can throw away. As you do this, imagine that the stress or worry or other bad emotion is leaving at the same time.

How to Confront Your Feelings

The next thing to do is confronting the feelings that you have. You need to be able to actually identify your true emotions. Learning how to pinpoint and then name them makes it easier to control them. Take in a few breaths, and then take a look at the emotions and what you are feeling. Sometimes this will be painful, but it is imperative if you want to handle the emotions.

Once you face the emotions, think about what is causing them and whether they exist to cover up for something else that you are hiding from and afraid to confront.

Let's say that you need to take an exam, but that is making you feel stressed out. It may have a big impact on your future, or you may need to do well on this test to impress someone. You may feel nervous, but the root of this may be that you think the love of your family will depend on how successful you are. Naming your emotions is a skill that a lot of people have not learned how to do. It is a skill that will not only change your emotional intelligence but can also change your life and the way that you handle your emotions.

Remember that there is no such thing as a wrong emotion. If you are in the habit of telling yourself that an emotion is bad or that you shouldn't be feeling, it can cause you a lot of harm. Instead of doing this, notice the emotion without passing any judgment. Accept that all emotions are natural, and give yourself some time to feel it. This will give you a better chance to handle that emotion and get through it faster.

Next, you must give yourself permission to go through the emotion. It is a habit of most people to take their emotions and bottle them up, ignoring the emotions in hopes that they will go away. This never happens. These emotions may seem like they went away, but they will just resurface later on. Letting yourself feel these emotions can make a big difference in how long they stick around.

This doesn't mean that you have to focus on the emotions all the time—but if you feel a particularly tough emotion, then set aside a bit of time each day to help get that emotion out. If you are upset, you can take some time to cry. If you feel angry, envious, or stressed, you can do something physical to work it out. Or you can write out the emotions to get them out of you.

From here, you need to think about what you can do to help resolve that situation. Sometimes you may feel like your emotions are out of control because you aren't sure how to handle your life's circumstances. This can lead to some sort of a broken record on repeat where you obsess about your negative thoughts in a way that is already bad for you. It is important to break off this cycle by focusing on any part of the situation that you can actually control.

Instead of wasting your time thinking about the trouble, think about all the things that you are able to control. Hence, instead of focusing your attention on being bad at your job, consider asking someone for help to do a better job at work, find some better stress management techniques, and ask your boss how you could be more productive on the job. You won't be able to control everything about the situation, but sometimes being able to control just a few things can make a big difference.

Healthy Ways to React to Your Emotions

It is important that you learn how to react to your emotions in a way that is safe and healthy. This can be hard to learn, but it is a sign of higher emotional intelligence. The first thing to focus on is to recognize when defensiveness is occurring in others and in yourself. Defensiveness is an emotion that not only leads you to emotions that are out of control but can also make it such that other people think you are too emotional. There are a lot of reasons why you may feel defensive. You may be frustrated or stressed, or feel like someone is personally attacking you.

There are a number of signs that you are being defensive. These can include:

- Using criticism towards the other person to deflect any criticism, even if it is constructive, from you.
- Ignoring good feedback from others.

- Listing out the reasons why you're right without getting the opinion of others.
- Smiling and nodding just to get the other person to stop talking to you.
- Crossing your arms and working to shut the other person out.
- Passing blame to someone else.
- Making excuses for your own failures.
- Refusing to listen to any feedback that is negative or doesn't match up with what you want to hear.

It is also important to know your own emotional triggers. Triggers are going to be any events, places, things, people, or activities that will consistently bring out an emotion in you. When it comes to negative emotions, it is your job to take precautionary measure against things that may trigger them any further.

For example, say that every time you see a family member, they end up making you angry and frustrated. Before going to the next family gathering, you may do some self-care to help you relax. You may come up with a plan to take some breaks from that family member throughout the day. You can even limit the time that you spend with that family member and make plans to leave the gathering early if needed. This helps you control your anger and still have a good time.

Next, you need to learn how to do nothing when you feel someone is aggravating you. There are times when people will try to get a rise out of you. Instead of getting angry, take a deep breath, and speak in a calm manner—refusing to let anyone get to you. When you remain calm and collected, the other person is going to get frustrated that you aren't responding, and they will give up.

Any time that you start to feel upset or angry about a situation, implement some relaxation techniques. Letting the emotions flow out without any changes can end up making that emotion grow even more. Consider trying something that is the opposite of what you normally do. If you often get bothered when your spouse doesn't finish the dishes, challenge yourself to complete the dishes on your own, then politely see if your spouse will be willing to help.

When a strong emotion hits you, the last thing you want to do is think of the opposite thing and then follow through. It will take some time, and there will be instances when you will struggle. However, keep working on it. With a little bit of practice, you will be surprised at how quickly you can turn that negative emotion around.

Finally, if you feel that you are in a situation that is bringing out some negative feelings, then it is time to remove yourself right away. The best reaction in many cases is to just walk away and avoid those triggers altogether. If you are able to rework the situation easily without causing harm to others, you can remove yourself, so that you can get away from the negative feelings and keep the emotions in check.

A good example of this is if you are on a committee at work. The other people in that group are unfocused and just don't want to concentrate on the work at hand, and this can make any meeting with them frustrating. One thing that you can consider doing if it is allowed, is to ask if you can be assigned to a different committee.

When those negative emotions start to come up, it is important to find a healthy way to deal with that emotion. Whether it is to recognize that emotion and direct it somewhere else, to remove yourself from the situation, or to figure out the opposite reaction than your normal and then choose to go with that one, you must make sure that those emotions stay under your control.

Simple Steps to Help You Control Your Emotions

Being able to control your emotions can be difficult. You are going to experience emotions—no matter how hard you try to avoid them—and there are times when those emotions will try to get the best of you. Some of the simple steps that you can follow to control your emotions include:

- Try not to react right away: Reacting right when something happens that turns you on emotionally can be a bad mistake. When you let this happen, you will probably do or say something that you will regret later. Before you let the emotion take over, take in a deep breath and try to stabilize those impulses. Continue the deep breathing for the next five minutes, focusing on getting the muscles to relax and get the heart rate back to normal. As you calm down, affirm that these emotions are normal but only temporary.

- Ask for guidance from the divine: No matter what religion you follow, developing a good relationship with the divine can help you to get over obstacles that get in your way much better. This is because those who believe in a higher force believe that there is divine intervention that will show them the way to go.
- Find a healthy way to let those emotions out: Now that you have found some ways to manage your emotions, it is time to find ways to release those that are healthy and productive. Never bottle up the ones that you have because this will just result in a blow out later on. Talk to someone about the emotions, keep a journal, do some aggressive exercise, or find something that helps you get rid of those emotions productively.
- Look at the bigger picture: Everything that goes on in our lives will serve a higher

purpose, whether these situations are good or bad. Wisdom means that you are able to see past these moments. Over time, you will start to see the bigger picture of the situation and may realize that your original reaction to the situation was unwarranted.

- Replace the thoughts you have: Many of us have programmed our brains to think in negative terms, but negative emotions are going to mean more negative thoughts—and this is a vicious cycle that is hard to get rid of. Whenever you are dealing with an emotion that makes you feel bad or have a negative thought, make a conscious effort to replace it with a more positive thought. Imagine the ideal resolution of your problem playing out or think about something or someone who can bring a smile to your face.
- Learn and forgive the emotional triggers: Each person has their own emotions

triggers, things that can make them tick in no time. No matter what the emotional trigger is, it is time to forgive them and let them go. Sometimes it is possible to walk away and avoid the triggers. If you can, then do this. But if not, learn how to forgive them and move on.

Emotions are going to be there no matter who you are. Those who may seem to have no emotions are simply those who have learned how to properly control them and can release them in a more productive manner. Use the ideas in this chapter to help you develop a higher emotional intelligence by increasing the control you have over your own emotions.

Chapter 5: Learn How to Read Emotions

A major component of your emotional intelligence is being able to read the emotions of others. There are different cues that people send out that can hold more meaning than just the words they say. We are often so caught up in what is going on in our own lives or too busy concentrating on how we will reply to others that we can miss out on these cues. By looking at the body language, the facial expressions, the tone of voice, and the words that are said, we can easily tell the emotion of the other person.

The culture and the language of a person are also going to influence how people will express their emotions. Despite these differences, all humans can experience some similar emotions. Their ability to read these emotions and then respond to them properly can really help them develop their emotional intelligence. Let's take a look at some of the things that a person can do to help read the emotions of those around them.

Analyzing the Emotions That Others Have

The first thing that you need to explore is the different emotions that people around you are expressing. First, we are going to recognize the differences between the positive and the negative emotions. No matter where someone comes from, there are six emotions that are seen as universal. These include disgust, sadness, fear, anger, surprise, and happiness. As you can see from the list, these fall into two main categories—namely, positive and negative.

In order to identify these emotions in others, you need to know what behaviors and actions are associated with each of the categories of emotions. These will include:

- The positive emotions have the power to reduce stress, increase your awareness and your memories, and can really improve the mood. These emotions are going to include emotions like relief, inspiration, confidence, courage, love, kindness, sympathy, surprise, and happiness.
- The negative emotions, on the other hand, will do the opposite. They are there to help you deal with any situation that feels challenging, allow you to recognize when there may be something threatening to you and can increase your stress levels. Some of the emotions that fall into this category include disgust, contempt, anger, fear, and sadness.

While understanding the two types of emotions can be important, you need to be able to learn when someone is experiencing one or the other. The first place to look is at the mouth or the eyes.

The region that the person uses can depend on where they are from and their culture. For example, if you are in Japan, you would want to focus more on the eyes. If you are in the United States, you would want to focus more on the mouth or the whole face to see which emotions may be there.

In either case, stand far enough that you are able to get a good look at the face of the person you are talking with, but make sure you are still close enough to carry on a conversation. This helps you take in the whole face and better discern which emotions exist.

The tone of voice can also be important in determining which emotions are present. People can use their voice to show and control their emotions. There are some emotions that aren't shown through the tone of voice very well. Some emotions, like confidence, contentment, boredom, stress, and relaxation can be shown through the voice pretty well. Other emotions, like sadness, happiness, friendliness, and fear are sometimes hard to catch based on the tone of voice.

There are also times when a similar tone of voice can be used to express different types of emotions. A tense or a harsh voice is going to be associated with different emotions like interest, confidence, hostility, and anger. A tone of voice that is more whispery or soft tone can be counted with a wide range of emotions like boredom, sadness, friendship, intimacy, contentment, and relaxation—but going with a soft or breathy voice can be with nervousness, shyness, and fear.

In addition to looking at the tone of voice, you should note the demeanor and the behavior of the person you are communicating with. Does the other person look friendly or are they more reserved? Sometimes the emotion can be experienced in more of an unconscious manner, without you really understanding how you are aware of it. Using your best judgment and trusting the gut can sometimes be one of the most accurate ways to read emotions.

For example, you can recognize emotion in others simply by noting how you react to them. It is common to mirror the emotions of others. This means that if someone is angry or sad or happy, you may be mirroring, or copying, those emotions and portraying it back to them. You can do this in your behavior, tone of voice, or facial expressions.

You will quickly find that emotions can be contagious. You're often going to be affected by the emotions that others are feeling. Even if you are in a good mood, it is possible to become sad or frustrated based on how those around you are feeling. This is why it's more likely for you to smile back if someone does smile at you while passing.

The physical well-being of the other person is also an indicator of their emotions. Emotions are able to physically influence the health of the individual. Sometimes this is in a positive manner, such as when the person is positive, upbeat, and happy. Other times it is in a negative manner, such as when the person is sad or depressed. If you notice that the other person seems to be sick or tired all the time, then maybe they are experiencing depression or stress.

The next step is to develop and then improve your emotional intelligence. The best way to start recognizing emotions in others is to start being more aware of all the emotions around you. There are four branches of emotional intelligence, and all of them are very important when increasing your EQ. The four branches include:

- Being able to perceive and recognize the different emotions that not only others are feeling but also the emotions that you are feeling.

- Being able to use these emotions to help promote thinking.
- Being able to understand the significance of each emotion.
- Being able to manage these emotions.

There are many different things that you can do to help improve your emotional intelligence and make it easier to understand how others are feeling. These strategies include:

- Put away the technology. You need to work on your social skills, not your social media skills. Face-to-face communication is one of the best ways to learn how to read nonverbal cues and learn about emotions.
- Allow the negative and uncomfortable feelings to come around. No one wants to experience them, but they are chances to learn and grow. Instead of getting upset about these emotions, figure out why you are feeling these emotions in the first

place, and think of a way how you can avoid them in the future.
- Always listen to your body: The knot in your stomach can be telling you something important.
- Ask for someone to help you recognize the emotions if you are running into trouble there.
- Keep a record of your thoughts and feelings. This can make a difference as you learn how to manage your emotions.

How to Interpret Facial Expressions

Facial expressions are a great way to read the emotions that others are sending your way. Sometimes the words and the facial expressions aren't going to match up, and you may need to dig deeper and ask more questions to figure out what is really going on. On the other hand, the facial expressions may add more meaning to how the other person feels. Either way, you must take the time to learn how to read facial expressions if you want to start recognizing emotions.

The first step is to just make an active choice to recognize facial expressions. Sometimes the real emotions that we feel will be expressed in the eyes and on our faces. Being able to learn the different facial expressions and how they relate to different emotions can make it easier to recognize what emotions are going on.

Reading facial expressions can take some time. There are some people who are really good at changing their facial expressions to hide the emotions that they are experiencing. They may look happy based on their facial expressions, but they are actually sad or angry. You may have to rely on other cues to help you here, such as their tone of voice and their body language, to help you figure out what emotion is actually present.

Next, you need to have some practice recognizing when a smile is genuine or not. Sometimes people will try to hide their anger or their sadness with a smile, but when you are feeling these intense negative emotions, it is hard to show off a genuine smile. A genuine smile is going to use up a lot more muscles of the face compared to one that is forced or fake. The corners of the mouth should be up. Also, if you notice that the muscles that are near the eyes start to tighten, then this is a good sign that they are showing you a genuine smile.

You also need to learn how to distinguish sadness from happiness. This one might seem like an obvious one to work on, but people who try to control or hide their true emotions are able to smile even when they feel sad. Emotions that are genuine can be hard to fake, though. For example, sadness can be associated with a lot of frowning and raising of the inner corners of the eyebrows. You may also see things like drooping eyelids that cover up the eye a little bit.

In the business world, if you have someone who is angry or disgusted with you, this is not a good thing—and if you are not able to recognize the signs of this, you can quickly turn your customers off of you and can get yourself into some sticky situations. Anger and disgust are often associated together, and they are going to have similar facial expressions. Many times, when you are annoyed, angry, or disgusted, you will wrinkle up your nose, for example.

Often feelings of resentment and anger are going to be towards something or someone. When you are angry, you are going to down the eyebrows, purse the lips, and bulge the eyes. If you see these signs, especially if they are all together, then this means that the other person is probably resentful or angry towards you.

You will find that some other negative feelings, like disdain, disgust, or dislike will be associated with some different signals. A loose lower lip and a raised upper lip will often come with these emotions. There will also be a little pulling down of the eyebrows, but not as much as when you see someone who is angry.

It is also possible to recognize when someone is experiencing feelings of surprise or fear. These are interesting emotions because even though one is positive and one is negative, they are both going to activate your sympathetic nervous system and can trigger that fight or flight response. When there is something unexpected that happens, no matter if it is a good thing or a bad thing, it will end up stimulating a part of the brain you have trouble directly controlling. When this happens, you are going to pull up the eyelids and the eyebrows, resulting in the eyes being wide open.

Even though both of these emotions can get the same parts of the brain and show themselves in similar ways, there are some differences. When someone is afraid, they are going to pull their eyebrows in towards the nose; their pupils will start to dilate to take in some more light; the mouth will be open, and many muscles of the face will start to tense up. When someone is surprised, they are more likely to drop the jaw and arch their eyebrows. The muscles near the mouth will be open and more relaxed.

Other Methods to Help You Read Emotions

There are also other signals that you can look at to figure out how someone is feeling. The first place to look here is at some of the nonverbal cues. In addition to the tone of voice and the facial expressions that we talked about above, you can look for some of the nonverbal cues that the person is sending to you. For someone who is not used to reading these nonverbal cues, they can end up being misleading. However, once you master these nonverbal cues, you can easily pick up on the emotions of the other person.

The right nonverbal cues are able to help convey the emotion of the other person. Some of the cues that you should look for include eye contact, posture, and body movement. For example, when you are talking to someone, check to see if they are stiff and tense or if they are more animated. Does the person stand up straight and put some effort into looking straight into your eyes; or do they hunch down, fidget with their hands, and cross their arms? Some important nonverbal signs you should look for include:

- Standing up straight and moving around will show that someone feels comfortable and open. If there are too many movements, such as the energetic waving of the arms, combined with a voice that is loud, it can show that someone is angry or excited.
- Hunched shoulders along with crossed arms and a voice that is quiet can show that someone is nervous or uncomfortable.

If that person is not able to make eye contact with you, it can mean that they feel guilty or upset about something.
- There are also different cultural and social situations that will factor into this. For example, in the United States and Europe, eye contact is important and a sign of respect. However, for those in African and Asian cultures, it is aggressive or rude.

The posture and the body movements of the other person can tell you a lot about their emotional state. While looking at their face can provide you with a lot of information, you should also look at the entire body of the person you are studying. Body movements and posture can also help you know how intense the emotion is. Some parts of the body that you must pay attention to in order to learn the emotions of the other person include:

- The torso and the shoulders: If the person is leaning forward or hunching their shoulders, this often means that they are angry. If they are leaning back, it can be more of a sign of fear or panic. If the person is standing up straight, having their head high and shoulders back, then this can show that they are confident. If they are nervous, bored, or looking for sympathy, the other person may slump themselves forward.

- Hands and arms: If the other person is sad, they will have their arms next to their sides with the hands inside the pocket. If they are irritated or annoyed, they can take one arm and keep it near the hips or the side and then gesture with the other hand, usually with the palm flat or pointing. When the other person doesn't care or feels indifferent, then both the hands will stay behind their back.

- Feet and legs: You can even look at the feet and legs of the other person to gauge their emotions. If they are tapping their toes or shaking their legs, this is a sign that they are annoyed, anxious, or in a hurry.

Recognizing some of the signs of fight or flight can be important as well. When the body is in this mode, it is usually going to result in the person feeling anxious, stressed, or nervous. When this happens, you may notice that their hands are shaking, they have a flushed face that is red, or they have sweaty palms. When men are feeling stressed and upset, you must look for signs of anger, frustration, or aggression. Women are a bit different because they are likely to turn to social support or become more talkative. Some personalities can become quiet or withdrawn when they go through emotions that are more negative.

No matter what the other person is feeling, you can always ask them how they are. This is the most direct method to use, although the other person may not be as honest as you may expect. Sometimes they will say they are fine, but asking never hurts. And it may give you some clues, such as tone of voice, into how they are actually feeling.

Speaking to the other person on their own, rather than trying to do it in front of a large group, can help. This often encourages the other person to be more open, and they are less likely to be embarrassed by the answer they give.

In most cases, you will need to work through several different signals to figure out the emotions that the other person is feeling. Sometimes the tone of voice or the expressions on the face will be enough for this. But often you will need to combine the signals to get a good feeling for how the other person is doing.

Reading the emotions of others can be an important part of your emotional intelligence. This is true whether you are able to get them to talk directly to you, or you have to go through all the different cues above to get the answers. Once you are able to recognize an emotion, then you are more likely to recognize it and learn how to take control of it. Whether you are experiencing the emotion for yourself, or you are trying to learn how to read the emotions of others, these are skills that will help you improve your emotional intelligence.

Chapter 6: Learn How to Analyze People

As you work on your emotional intelligence, there will be times when you need to analyze other people. This will ensure that you are able to understand what the other person is feeling and what makes them tick, and it can help you interact with them a bit better.

You are probably already spending time analyzing people, but you do so for some of the superficial qualities, rather than the ones that provide a real sense about the people you want to analyze. You may analyze to figure out if they seem nice or if you will want to spend time with them, but with only a few minutes to do this process, how much information are you actually going to be able to glean from them? Will you actually be able to learn about them on a deep level with these few minutes? Probably not.

The first thing you need to do is figure out some of the clues to look for in order to better analyze people. You don't always have a lot of time to get this analysis done. Sure, you can spend some time analyzing a new neighbor or coworker. But if you are analyzing a client and need to make a sale quickly, that time frame is going to be much smaller. Some of the clues you can follow to help guide your analysis of someone include:

The Words That They Say

During this step, you need to develop an interest in what people are talking about. The topics that people like to bring up will provide you with a lot of insight into what they find valuable. Some people will talk about their health or their spiritual matters. Some will talk about sports or school. Some like to talk about their families and their kids. No matter what someone wants to talk about, these words really provide hints about the behaviors and mind-thought processes of the individual. This means that you are able to form an analysis about the way people behave based on what they say.

Another thing you can watch out for is the tone of voice an individual uses towards others. The tone of voice has a big effect on how you will communicate. Some of the best orators have been able to master the art of moving people and convincing them to do things. Soft-toned people may indicate that the person is shy or that they are tired. Loud-toned people are more likely to be for those who are more aggressive or those who want to be in charge.

The way that a person talks, as well as the words that they say, can really reveal a lot about them. It can show you how people are reacting to certain situations, how they play a part, and what is the most important thing in the world to them. Recognizing these patterns can help you better analyze anyone you come across.

Look at Any Reactions That Are Spontaneous

When you are looking at the behavior of an individual, make sure to look out for some actions that don't seem scripted. Many people know how they are supposed to act in public. They know that even if they are stressed or worried or sad or angry that going around with these emotions on their sleeves isn't a good thing in public. But that doesn't mean they can conceal these emotions or thoughts all the time.

When the person does blunder that you notice, take note of how they react to that. Does the person try to conceal that the blunder happened, or do they just smile about it and move on? Did the person even notice that they did the blunder? These behaviors can help you know what type of individual you are dealing with in terms of how they like being viewed by others and their self-confidence. Even things like the way they cough, sneeze, or even take care of their appearance can tell you a ton about them.

How They Present Themselves and Their Fashion Sense

The next thing that you can look at is the tastes and the preferences of the individual you are around. You should look at how they handle the trends in fashion—if they like to have vintage clothes, a mix of fashion, or something else. Even the fashion statements and the way a person presents themselves when they go out in public can really showcase the behaviors and mannerisms of the person. For example, frequently wearing dark clothes, sunglasses, and other similar clothing can show that the person doesn't really reveal their personal life to many people.

In the same idea, you can take some time to gauge their vanity affinity. Are they obsessed with how other people view them when they wear certain clothes? Do they like to spend a lot of time looking in the mirror to make sure they still look good? This can also tell a lot about the behavior of a person.

Personal Space

The amount of personal space that the person likes can tell you a lot about them. Some people don't mind being near others, and they have very small personal bubbles. These people are often lively, outspoken, and ready to be friends with everyone. There are also those who like to have a lot of personal space. They are more reserved and can get uncomfortable if someone gets too close to them. Most people will fall somewhere in between.

Analyze the Body Language

Body language is the biggest indicator that can help you analyze another person. Subconsciously, you will send out signals through your body that others can look at and interpret to mean something extra or in addition to the words that you are speaking. For example, you may say that you agree with someone else, but if you grimace or roll your eyes, then you may be seen as insincere.

Eye contact is a great example of using body language to read someone. Do you notice that someone always seems to avert their eyes when you ask a question that needs an honest answer? Do you notice that someone shifts their eyes or has trouble making direct eye contact when they talk to someone? This can be a sign that the other person doesn't have a lot of self-confidence, or that they are not honest with the answers that they give.

The composure of the other person can be crucial as well. People who are relaxed and comfortable with themselves and the conversation will adapt more of a position that is a standstill. But those who are anxious may tap their feet or be really fidgety. If they fold their arms across their chest, they may seem like they are more defensive or that they are not going to be open about their responses—while holding the hands at the back can show that the person is more open. You can even find out a lot about someone based on their walk. Someone who has a bit of a swag or pomp is more likely to have a lot of power and confidence compared to those who drag their feet or walk with less certainty.

The neat thing about looking at body language is that it is less likely to lie to you compared to the words that someone tells you. It is best to believe the body language of a person when you are in doubt about what they are telling you. As you get better at reading body language, you will be able to really learn about the other person, even if they don't directly tell you something.

Some of the Do's When Profiling People

If you wish to give yourself an accurate report on the behavior of a person, then you should do a few things to make sure that your work is not compromised. You want to come up with a good analysis of a person based on the signs that are in front of you, without any judgment or looking at the information the wrong way. Some of the pointers that you can follow to help you do a good job of analyzing the behavior of other people include:

- Be keen: You need to always be observant when you are trying to pick up vital pieces of information. If you find that you are talking a lot, then maybe it is time to spend more time watching and listening to people near you. The biggest reason that many people fail at being able to read others is they are not keen observers.

- Learn to sieve and separate: After you get some practice with this, you can then train yourself to have sharper senses. You can do this so well that it will become easy to note the differences and similarities in how someone behaves. You can start to detect even the smallest details about people's tendencies and similarities.
- Make contact: If you want to be able to read other people, you need to be able to engage with them. This doesn't always need to be a conversation. A simple smile, a comment about the weather, or a casual glance can be enough to get this contact. From these simple gestures, you can then build up to starting a conversation with the person. Perhaps you will communicate by revealing yourself to the people you interact with. Then share something that you either like or dislike with that person, something about work, a song, or something else. Then you can ask them

their opinion and build up the conversation from there. This helps you warm up the conversation and build a relationship with them.

- Empathize rather than sympathize: The ability to see the world from the perspective of other people can be a useful tool when you want to analyze the behavior of someone. You will be able to empathize with them when you can put yourself in their shoes and imagine how they would react to certain events or actions. Different people have their own pasts and their own stories, and this means they are going to react differently than you may to a situation. To grow your emotional intelligence, you need to be able to grow your empathy to understand how other people react and why they may behave in a certain way.

- Approximate and guestimate: To do a good job at reading the minds of others, try to approximate and guess the reactions that are bound to come from people when they enter into different circumstances. A near-correct guess, while not perfect, will actually do a lot to pointing you in the right direction. As you get some more practice with this, you will be able to eliminate how many guesses you need to do so that you can make good guesses on how to interact with that person.

- Learn how you can be a database: When you are analyzing the behavior of a person, you should collect as much information as possible. Learn the general and the specific behaviors of people. But you do want to be careful when storing and retaining information so you don't end up with judgments that are unfounded against people. Store only the information that you see as valuable instead of letting yourself be misled by the information that you found.

- Be patient: Remember that it is going to take a lot of time to master any skill. And the skill of reading people will take even longer to master. If you just to make these judgments with just a few minutes of conversation and interaction with other people, then you are going to be wrong with your guesses. Take enough time to gather information that can really aid you in making solid conclusions about the other person. With enough practice, you are going to be able to learn how to accurately read the people around you.

Some of the Don'ts When Profiling People

While there are a few things that you can do to ensure you accurately analyze the people you meet, there are also a few things that you should avoid. Avoiding these things is important because it ensures that you get an accurate read on someone, rather than just following the judgments in your head or the stereotypes that are there from other situations. Some of the things that you should make sure you avoid doing when analyzing people include:

- Don't stereotype: At all times, you must avoid stereotyping the people that you meet and stay away from any myths that you may have heard in the past. For example, there is a common thought or myth that those who have unkempt hair are dangerous, which is not really true. You shouldn't base your predictions on any of the myths that you may have heard in the past. Everyone is different and listening to these stereotypes and myths can make you greatly misjudge someone.
- Never take a side: It is best to stay neutral when you are doing your analysis. This helps you to appreciate that each person is going to be different and each one has a different point of view. Try to avoid any

fixed or rigid expectations and be as accommodative as possible. This is definitely where that empathy from earlier can come into play when you are trying to analyze the people around you.

- Judge characters rather than positions: It is easy to pass certain people because we are either intimidated by them or because we admire them. This can include anyone who is in a higher position. We may give them a lot of desirable qualities without even knowing them, and this can really cause bias to the judgment that we have. It is much better to learn about each individual person, regardless of what their background, to ensure that you learn about them and what is important to them, rather than what you think they must put a priority on.
- Don't be clouded by your emotional state: When you are working to read the mannerisms and behavior of people, it is

important that you keep your heart open and your mind clear. Your emotional state is so important since adding your own emotions to the mix can make it easier to make mistakes when you overlook obvious facts. Before you get started with analyzing someone else, be aware of your own emotional state.

Analyzing people can be difficult. It may take you some time to get your feet wet with this step and to help you see results. There are times when you will analyze people, especially in the beginning, and you will be wrong, but keep practicing. This is the only way that you will get better at analyzing—and once you get it down, you can easily use it to help you any time that you interact with another person in the future.

Chapter 7: Think Like an Empath

Empathy is basically the ability to feel what other people around you do. This is a huge key to forming meaningful relationships and to coexist in a peaceful manner with others. There are some people who seem to be born with the natural ability to empathize with others, while there are others who find it hard to relate to those around them. Nevertheless, if you find that your ability to put yourself in the shoes of others seems to be lacking a bit, there is some good news. This chapter is going to talk about the meaning of empathy a bit more while providing you with the tips you need to become a more empathetic person.

The Importance of Thinking like an Empath

There are a lot of benefits that come with thinking like an empath. While there is often a misconception that empaths are easily offended, feel too deeply, and are overly sensitive—this is not the case. An empath simply is better able to connect with others because they can read emotions and know how to understand what the other person is feeling. When it comes to your emotional intelligence and reaching your goals, this can be a good thing.

Some of the benefits that you will start to see in your daily life when you work towards being an empath include:

- You can always tell who is telling you the truth.
- Any time that you feel happy, rest assured that you *are* truly happy.

- Empaths can feel emotions really well. This means that when something excites them, it can really make their whole day and give them something big to look forward to.
- If there is something going on that doesn't make you feel right, as an empath, you are probably right about it.
- You can tell when someone is feeling sad, depressed, or anxious. You can even understand why they may be feeling these emotions and will be comfortable enough to help them out.
- Empaths are better at knowing the right things to say. They know the emotions that are going on with the other person, and so they won't stumble and say something wrong. This can go a long way with them comforting another person, but it can also help them get ahead because they can say the right thing to the right people at the right time.

- You can easily tell when someone is upset. An empath will then know if they must just stay away from that person and let the emotion fizzle out or if they should try to resolve that emotion before things get out of hand.
- Empaths seem to be able to tell better when someone is sick. Often this occurs because the empath is going to take on the illness and those feelings, at least a little bit when they are around that person.
- Empaths are better at knowing how to treat other people. This is because they are aware of how those actions can make them feel, and they don't want to do the same to someone else.
- Relationships with an empath are more open and honest. This is because the empath can usually tell when the other person is lying to them. They will seek out those who don't lie to them and hold onto those relationships.

- Empaths are more in touch with their environment. When someone is upset, they can be there and try to take care of it. They are easily able to shift their actions accordingly to fit into the new environment. This adaptability is something that a lot of people struggle with, but empaths can use this to get themselves ahead.
- Empaths have a good understanding of how they interact with others. They are more careful about these interactions because they understand how everything is connected and try to keep it in balance.
- As an empath, you can easily tell when someone or something feels off. You can know this right away without any intuitive training. This helps you stay away from the wrong people and can change the way that your life goes.

How to Increase Your Empathy

Increasing your empathy is something that a lot of people wish they could do. They want to form those deep connections with other people. They want to be able to read others better. They may just want to understand what others are thinking better. Some of the things you can do to help increase your empathy for others include:

Tapping into your empathy

First, you need to learn how to get in touch with the emotions that you have. If you can't control or understand the emotions that come from within, then how are you going to understand the emotions of other people? Are you already tuned into the feelings and emotions that you have, or do you need to work on them? Do you notice when your feelings change and if you are feeling afraid, angry, happy, or sad? Do these feelings come up to the surface? Do you allow yourself to express these emotions?

If you find that you try to tamper down the emotions, or you tend to push them down rather than expressing them, then it is time to become more of an empath. This means that you need to let yourself feel more deeply.

It is common for a lot of people to push aside some of the negative feelings that they are going for. If you feel angry or sad, it may seem like a good idea to try and distract yourself with watching a show or going out to the bar drink rather than thinking about the issue that caused the emotion. But when you push these feelings aside, you are disconnecting. If you aren't able to express your own emotions, no matter what they are, how are you going to feel the emotions from someone else?

If you do struggle with this point, then it is time to give your emotions some free reign. Set aside a bit of time each day so that the emotions can come to the surface. Instead of letting your natural instincts push those negative feelings down, take the time to think through them. If you are angry, afraid, or some other negative emotion, take the time to deal with it in a healthy way. This will do so much for helping you get in touch with your emotions.

Next, you need to learn how to listen carefully. It is too easy to get caught up in what is going on around us, in our own little world. Think about a time when you really listened to a story that moved you. Were you able to forget yourself? Were you able to see yourself as a character in the story, wondering what would happen next? This is the way that you must listen to anyone you communicate with. Rather than thinking about your own problems or worrying about what you will say back, just listen to what they tell you. You will be surprised at what you are able to hear.

Not only should you take some time to listen to the other person and put yourself in their shoes—you also need to show how you feel for them. Ask questions when they are talking to show that you are listening to them. Use the right body language to show that you are engaged. This means to lean into them a little, to make eye contact, and to try to limit your fidgeting. These are methods that show that you are empathetic to the other person right in that moment, and they do wonders for building up trust with the other person.

Of course, you can also share about yourself as well. People like to feel that they are your confidant as well, rather than just being the only one to talk. Making yourself vulnerable with the other person, just like you expect them to do with you, can help open up those lines of communication and build the trusting relationships you are looking for.

How to grow your empathy

All of us start out with some degree of empathy. The levels may not be where we want them, but we at least have some. We know that some people have a hard time in life, and we may feel for them. If we hear a story about a baby who was harmed in an accident, we are going to feel for the baby and all the suffering they are going through. We will feel for the parents having to see their child go through all this. However, when it comes to feeling empathy for those we see and interact with on a daily basis, we may fall short on occasion.

The first thing you can do to build up your empathy is to be open to learning about things that maybe you don't understand completely. Empathy is going to come from a natural desire to know more about other people and their experiences. If you want to grow your empathy, then you need to start being more curious about how life is like for those who are different from you. Make it a point to learn as much as you can about new things each day. Some of the ways that you can put that curiosity to work include:

- Spend more time traveling: When you visit new places, take the time to meet the people who live there, getting to know about them and the way they live their lives.
- Talk to strangers: If you are sitting on the bus, in a waiting room, or somewhere else, try starting up a conversation with that person rather than looking at your phone or in a book.
- Try something outside of your routine. If you have a tendency to go to the same places and hang out with the same people, then it may be time to mix it up. This helps you expand your horizons and meet new people.

Another option is to practice empathy with those around you. If you are new to this process, try practicing it with people you know and trust. You already have a predisposition to these people and their feelings, so having some empathy towards them will not be so hard. You can practice and work on your skills this way and build up to showing empathy to others.

Over time, you can build up and start showing empathy to other people. How easy is it to show empathy to people you have just met and know nothing about? How easy is it to show empathy to people you don't really like? These are all areas you can explore as you try to increase your emotional intelligence.

How to Think More like an Empath

Those who have a lot of empathy do a good job with their emotional intelligence. The ability to walk in the shoes of someone else and to connect with others on an emotional level can do so much to help you out with this emotional intelligence. Someone who is an empath knows what it is like to feel and see things in a way that others don't. In fact, empaths have a great ability to really understand other people, whether they have known this person for a long time or if they have just met that person. While others struggle with social norms and getting to know someone else, empaths have the ability to connect with someone right away, no matter the situations.

This is something that is unusual in our modern world. Too many times we get stuck in our own little worlds, looking on our computers, paying attention to the phone, or just spending all our time thinking about our own problems or our own replies to what someone is saying. We just don't know how to properly connect to others who are around us.

But an empath is often different. They know how to connect with people, even if those people seem to have nothing in common with them. The empath seems to have the innate ability to connect with others and understand why someone acts in a certain way, and they can walk a mile in that person's shoes.

If you want to increase your emotional intelligence, you need to learn how to think like an empath. For some people, this can take a lot of time. They may be so caught up in their own worlds and their own problems that they aren't sure how to handle thinking about someone else or realizing why someone else reacts a certain way. The good news is that you can take your time with this process. Even a slight improvement is better than nothing—and over time, your skills with empathy will get better.

So how do you turn your thinking around so you can be more empathetic to those near you? The following tips will help you get started:

Learn how to walk in others' shoes.

The most important thing you can do when working on your empathy is to learn how to walk in the shoes of others. It is hard to be empathetic and understanding of other people if you can't even imagine what they are going through. And there are so many different types of people, people who are different than what you are like, who sometimes hard to understand when it comes to their actions.

When you walk in someone else's shoes, you are allowing yourself to think like the other person. You imagine what they must go through during the day, what may be setting them off, or why they may see something as acceptable when you will never dream of doing the same.

For example, there are many different cultures in the world. What one culture considers polite, another may find rude. In the United States, it is common to make eye contact when speaking to someone. Failing to do this can be seen as rude and insensitive, or as though the person doesn't want to listen to what you have to say. But in some other cultures, including many Asian cultures, it is considered rude to make such direct eye contact. In this situation, one party can see the other as being disrespectful while for another, they are being polite. Understanding these cultural differences and the meanings behind certain characteristics can make a big difference in how well you understand other people.

Another example is if someone comes up to you and starts yelling or sniping at you. Many times we assume the other person is mad at us, and this makes us frustrated as well. Instead of remaining calm, we get angry too and start sniping or yelling back, making the situation much worse and making everyone feel bad.

The better thing to do is to take a step back and realize that their anger probably isn't directed towards you. Perhaps they just got in a fight with someone else. Perhaps they had to drag the kids around all day and are worn out. Or they may just be having a bad day, and the frustration has finally built up. Seeing that other point of view and realizing that it is nothing personal towards you can help you take a different course of action, one that can possibly make the other person feel better.

Learn how to feel deeply.

Sometimes, we are scared of certain emotions showing up in our lives. We worry that we will feel bad about and will not be able to handle these emotions. We even worry that we are going to get hurt or made fun of because of them. This has forced us into a lifestyle where we try to ignore our feelings and push them down. The problem happens when our emotions start to come out because they refuse to be put down for so long.

It is not a bad thing to feel so deeply—it is human to feel deeply. You are not meant to keep your emotions hidden down. In fact, this is so bad for your health and emotional well-being. It often results in a big outburst because the emotions are tired of being put down so much. Finding constructive ways to deal with those deep feelings, and then allowing them to come out can really help when it comes to your emotional intelligence.

Listen to others because you care rather than because you have to.

Have you ever been in a conversation where you were trying to tell the other person something important, but they didn't seem to listen to you at all? What about a conversation where the other person was listening, but only because they had to and not because they really wanted to? How did this end up making you feel?

When you are listening to other people talk, it is imperative that you listen to them because you care to hear what they are saying. Just because they are your boss, your spouse, your kids, or someone else you feel like you have to listen to doesn't mean that you want to give them that kind of attention. When you listen to others because you care about them and about what they have to say, you will be amazed at the change.

The other person will feel more like you are truly listening to what they have to say. They will be excited to confide in you. You will hear things that you may have missed out on before. And you will be able to form a deeper bond with that person than ever.

Learn how to love serving others.

An empath is not just looking to understand the emotions of someone else; they also want to help that other person. When it comes to being empathetic and increasing your emotional intelligence, you have to realize that things are not always about you. You have to be willing to serve others and be there for them when they need it most.

Serving others can be such a beautiful thing. It helps others know that they can rely on you for help. It lets them know that they can confide in you and that you will be there. It helps them to feel loved, to get things done, and to feel like there is someone in the world on their side. And sometimes, this is all that people need in their lives.

Serving others can be beneficial to you as well. When you take the time to think about someone else and their needs, you are actually doing yourself a lot of good as well. Think about the last time you did a truly serviceable act, something to help out another person without looking to gain anything from it. How did you feel after the act was done? Pretty good, right?

When you add more serving of others to your daily life, you will be amazed at how much better you feel all the time. You will have happy emotions around you and have good emotions that can carry over to other parts of the day. For those who are dealing with a lot of negative emotions and trying to get them better under control to help their emotional intelligence, serving others is one of the best methods to make this happen.

Learn how to read people well.

We discussed this one in more depth in a previous chapter, but reading people can really go a long way towards you feeling empathetic. How are you supposed to feel for someone if you can't read them enough to know what emotions they are dealing with? If you are still uncertain about what you need to do to start reading people better, then it is time to revisit that chapter and get a little bit of practice in.

Create strong and lasting connections, even with those you haven't seen in a long time.

Those who are considered empaths are able to create strong and lasting connections. Even if they haven't seen someone for a long time, they know the importance of these strong and lasting connections. They make friends with someone, and they work to build up those bonds as much as possible. While others may make connections just to get themselves ahead in life, or because they are just near the other person without forming those deep connections, empaths can make bonds with people that never break.

These relationships are so beneficial in many different ways. They can help others feel more comfortable with you. It can help you to quickly learn how to read other people. It can help you to feel more connected with those who are around you. And when all these come together, you can live a more fulfilling life, both professionally and personally.

Learning how to think more like an empath can be so important. It allows you to truly understand what the other person is thinking and feeling so that you can connect with them in a much better way than you ever had. Take the time to follow the steps above, and you will be able to see some great results in no time with your emotional intelligence.

Things to Remember About Empathy:

- You are sharing someone's emotions: When you are feeling empathy, you are basically feeling the emotions of another person. This means that you need to go to a new level with that person—not just scratching the surface, but really getting to the bottom of who that person is. It can also be a shared understanding between you and the other person.
- You can feel empathy towards anyone, no matter the circumstances: It doesn't matter if you know the person really well or if you just met them. It doesn't even matter if you like the other person or not. You can feel empathy towards everyone you meet.

- You don't have to agree with someone to feel empathy for them: Just because you are empathetic towards someone doesn't mean you have to always agree with them. You can respect where they get their opinions and why they may feel a certain way, but that doesn't mean you have to just turn around give up the beliefs that you stand for. You do need to respect their right to an opinion, but as an empath, you can still uphold your own principles.

Chapter 8: Use Manipulation and Persuasion for Success and Mastery

As you work on your emotional intelligence, you will gain better control over your own emotions. Many of us have a lot of emotions during the day. These emotions are either right at the surface—ready to burst out at the worst possible time—or we bury them deep for a long time as they eat us up inside. Neither of these is a healthy method of dealing with our emotions, both negative and positive.

With a high EQ, it is easier to deal with these emotions. You have learned that the emotions are not something to be upset about or something that you need to push way down deep. Your emotions are valid, and it is fine to feel them. However, you need to take this a step further and find healthy and constructive ways to deal with those emotions, rather than letting them fester. A good emotional intelligence will help you to do this.

You will find that it is much easier to get a good read on other people. You can tell when they are feeling sad or happy or any other emotion out there. Even when the other person is telling you one thing, you can look at their posture, their hand signals, their facial expressions, and even their tone of voice to figure out if they are telling you the truth, or if there is some other emotion at play. You can even use this to bring out some strategies to help turn a bad or sad mood around.

So what can you do with all these skills that you have learned in this guidebook? This is where the ideas of persuasion and manipulation can come into play. While these two words may seem like bad ones—thanks to the media and some movies out there—they are actually not that bad. If you convinced someone to go with you to a burger place for supper when they wanted tacos, this isn't necessarily evil, but you used persuasion and manipulation techniques to do this.

As you become better with emotions and reading other people, you will naturally start to be a better persuader or manipulator. You will recognize what will work on the people you encounter, and you can read the body language to figure out whether one of your techniques will work or not.

Let's say that you meet someone who seems to be a little shy and reserved. You can quickly find this out, as long as you have been practicing your techniques, after talking to them for a few minutes. Knowing that they are more reserved, you may not want to use techniques that are pushy. Instead, going with a strategy of being friends and being on their side can really ensure you get the results that you want.

With both manipulation and persuasion, both of them are going to try to use reason in order to impress others into agreeing to your point of view. There are some differences between the two words, though, and knowing these can make a difference in how you may use them.

Let's start with persuasion. Persuasion is going to be the act of influencing someone towards a decision you want them to make. If you spend time explaining why a certain course of action is the right or logical one, and the person listening to you accept that point, then you were successful with your persuasion. On the other hand, if you did really well in school for a semester and tried to convince your parents to get you a car as a reward, then you are using persuasion as well.

Persuasion is unique because there is often some logic behind it. You must purchase this product because it makes your life easier. You must go to this place for supper because they are having a special. You did well on a test so you should be able to go out for the night. It isn't just you telling the other person something—there is some sound logic behind your reasoning, and that is why they are bound to follow you.

Many times salespeople will rely on persuasion to help get someone to purchase their product. They will generate a need for that service or product in the mind of their customer in hopes that the customer will succumb. If you are in sales, then you have used persuasion techniques on a daily basis in your work.

On the other, there is manipulation. Many people get the terms "manipulation" and "persuasion" mixed up. They are very similar, but with manipulation, you are taking advantage of how gullible someone is in hopes of deceiving them to agree with your personal point of view. While persuasion is beneficial to both parties, manipulation is not. Only the one manipulating others will benefit from this.

With persuasion, the salesperson will convince someone else to purchase the product. The person will get to leave with that product or service and can enjoy all the benefits from that product. The salesperson may get the benefit of making a sale and a little money in the process. This makes persuasion beneficial for both parties. With manipulation, the manipulator is going to try to control the other person to behave in a way that is mainly beneficial for the manipulator and no one else.

Often manipulation is seen as a bad thing because it is designed with the intent to deceive the other person. Surely, there are times when you can manipulate someone else and it may benefit them, but this is not the main focus of these techniques. With manipulation, the manipulator is trying to get all the benefits for themselves and isn't too concerned about how the other person would fair.

Now, when it comes to emotional intelligence, you will want to stick more with the persuasion techniques rather than manipulation.

Manipulation only benefits yourself, and it is only a short-term process. Even if you do see success with manipulation, the person may, after some time, catch on to who is manipulating them and who is just trying to persuade them. If you are caught manipulating them, you will lose the trust and the relationship bond that you worked so hard to get with that person.

Now, you can work with both of these techniques when you are using your emotional intelligence to get ahead. Remember that when you learn how to read people, you are opening yourself up to them and really start to understand them. This helps to build up a strong bond between you and the other person. They will trust you more, look to you for advice, and be willing to help you out. Even if you have just met the person, you can use their cues to help you figure out what makes them tick, so that you can successfully persuade them to act in a certain manner.

Common Persuasion Techniques to Help Change Anyone's Mind

There are a lot of persuasion techniques that you can rely on in order to get someone to follow the course of action that you choose. As you get better with your emotional intelligence and at reading people, you will be better equipped to recognize when you must use each of the following techniques. Some of the best persuasion techniques that you can utilize include:

Foot in the door

The foot in the door technique is one where, before you ask for a bigger favor from someone, you will start out by asking for a smaller one. When you ask for the first, smaller favor, you are getting the individual committed to helping you out. Then when that person is "on the hook" to help you, you can ask for the larger favor. At this point, the larger favor is more of a continuation of something the two of you technically agreed to.

The person will feel like since they already agreed to help you out, they may as well keep helping you here.

Some examples of how this may work in real life are below:

- A tourist stops you to ask for some directions. As a follow-up after you help them, they say that they may get lost on the way and then ask if you are able to walk them there. Since you have already helped them with the first request, you are more likely to walk them there than if they have immediately asked for that in the beginning.
- You missed out on a class because you were sick and then asked one of your classmates for their notes. After they agree to hand over the notes, you then admit that you have fallen a bit behind on the note-taking and ask if you can have some

of the notes for the last few classes. Because you asked for the smaller favor first, you will increase your chances of getting those other notes that you need.

So how effective is the foot in the door technique? In 1966, two researchers from Stanford decided to check this out. They took 156 women and separated them into four groups. They then called the first three of these groups and talked about some of their household kitchen products. Three days later, they asked these women to personally go through the kitchen cabinet and catalog the products that were there. The fourth group in this study were approached to look through the cabinet as well without having the initial phone call.

The first three groups had a compliance rate of 52.8 percent while the last group only had 22.2 percent. This shows that asking for the small favor, and then asking for the bigger one may not get you the results each time, but it is much better than asking for the big favor immediately.

Door in the face

The door in the face is the opposite of what we have talked about above. With this technique, you are going to ask the other person for something big, and when they say no, you will ask for something that is easier in comparison. Usually, the first thing that you ask for is not going to be something that you want, or at least not something that you will expect the other person to say yes to. The second request is the thing that you really want.

The idea here is that the other person may feel bad that they have to turn you down for the first request. Then when they hear the second request and how reasonable it sounds in comparison, they are more willing to complete it for you. If you haven't led off with the first request, then you will probably have a hard time getting them to agree to what you want to be done.

Some examples of how this may work in real life are below:

- You ask one of your classmates if they are willing to tutor you for the big exam that is coming up in Advanced Statistics that you haven't had any time to study for. The classmate says that they just don't have the time to help you out that much with all the stuff they need to get done. You can then follow up this original request by asking if they may share their notes with you. They are much more likely to agree to this.
- You ask a friend if you may be able to borrow $100. When they say no, you can ask if they may lend you $20.

Anchoring

The anchoring principle is more of a cognitive bias that is present in most decision making. For example, how can you tell whether a product is good or bad? Often you are going to compare it to a product that is similar and then base your decision from here. This technique can have a lot of different uses, and pricing is one of the more common. If you use anchoring in the proper way, it can be one of the best persuasion techniques.

Some examples of how this may work in real life are below:

- You are trying to purchase a new car. You find a deal that looks pretty good for about $10,000 on the vehicle that you want. You take some time to bargain with the salesman and get the price down to $7000. You go home and feel satisfied thinking that you have gotten the car for a great price since you talked the salesperson down so much. However, the actual value for the car is lower than $7000, but the salesperson told you the car was $10,000 as their anchoring point. That way, you would perceive anything that was lower than that amount as a good deal.

- You just got into a new job position that offered you $2000 per month. You end up negotiating with the human resources department and get your salary raised up to $2200. While this is a 10 percent raise, you have to take a look at how much that position is worth. If others in that position are making $3000 a month, then you really didn't do yourself a favor.

Commitment and consistency

You will find that most people are going to be prone to staying consistent with their beliefs and actions. If you are able to get someone to commit to something small, you can then take that relatively small commitment and influence them to do something bigger for you.

Some examples of how this may work in real life are below:

- Most of the time, you are likely to purchase the same brands over and over again. You know that you like them and that they are good products to work with. But when was the last time that you tried out something new or a different brand?
- "Can you do me a favor?" "Sure!" "Can you get me some beer from the store?" This works a lot better than just outright asking the person to grab the beverage for you.
- You have probably learned that sometimes goal setting can make productivity easier. The concept is something that is always present when you are trying to be successful. The reason that this is so effective is due to the consistency. This

helps you become more aware of what you want, and then you will strive to reach that.

Social proof

With this principle, you are going to rely on societal pressures to get the person to behave the way that you want. Most of your friends will pick out something, so you will do it too because if everyone else likes, trusts, or believes it, then it must be true.

You will find that social proof is one of the most common of the persuasion techniques. It doesn't take much to see that when there is a social group, there is a pretty high level of groupthink. Someone in the group is going to mention an idea, and then everyone else in the group will just go along with it. Even if it may not be your favorite thing to do or you don't want to do it, when you are in a social group, you will just agree to go along with it. This shows that when someone is trying to make a decision, many times they are going to look at how their peers are acting, and then do something similar.

Some examples of how this may work in real life are below:

- If you have a tip jar at work, you may want to consider putting a little bit of money inside before your shift begins. It has been shown that customers are more likely to leave a tip if they see that the jar is filled up, rather than seeing one that is empty. This is because many will assume that because others tip, they must do it as well.
- With social media, you are more likely to like a post that has a lot of other people liking it compared to a post that has zero likes.
- Even the likelihood of you smoking can be social proof. If everyone else around you, such as family and friends, take up

smoking, then it is more likely that you will smoke too even if you know the health concerns of doing this.

Authority

The next type of persuasion technique is authority. When you are able to put yourself out there as the expert or the authority on a subject, then you are more likely to get someone to act the way that you want. People seem to look up to those in authority in a field in order to get advice. They assume that these authority figures know what they are talking about and that they know what is best. So people will follow that advice. If you are successful at making yourself seem like an authoritative source, then people are more likely to listen and follow any advice that you give.

Some examples of how this may work in real life are below:

- Many smaller companies and even startups will put a logo that says "as seen on" on their landing pages any time they are featured on a major media website. This helps to show that they are kind of a big deal, even if you may not have heard of them yet.
- Many agencies will mention some of their previous clients on a landing page, especially if they have worked with some big companies in the past. This shows that they have some authority in the field and that others trust them, so you must too.

Scarcity

Nothing can persuade someone to do what you want more than the idea of scarcity. Scarcity is one of the most used techniques of persuasion that is out there, whether we are talking about marketers or salespeople. There are studies that show people tend to want more of things that seem to be in low supply. They worry that if they don't act now, that item may be gone for good, and they will never be able to get ahold of it again. If you are able to convince someone that your product or service is only available for a limited amount of time, or that you only have a limited supply of it, then it is more likely that they will want to get it before it's gone.

Some examples of how this may work in real life are below:

- Booking.com always makes it a point of theirs to show how there are only 2 to 3 rooms left in a hotel you are looking at, and there are also 20 more people looking at that hotel right now.
- Any product that is on the market that is a limited edition, only going to be out for a short amount of time, or has a limited-time price.

- Digital marketers will often make their own scarcity by offering a product once a year for a specific period of time while also stressing out how the product is a limited time offer. You can also see this when there is a discount on an item, but that discount only lasts for so long. The more you stress the limitations of the product and how long it will last, the higher the conversion rate.

Reciprocation

Finally, the last persuasion technique we will discuss is known as reciprocation. People often feel obliged to return any favors that are done for them. Regardless of whether that person actually likes the favor or the gift that you give, they still have some sort of inclination to give something in return. If you are able to get someone to feel indebted to you, then you can raise your chances of getting them to do something for your benefit.

Some examples of how this may work in real life are below:

- Let's say that you are doing some charity work for a cause that is close to your heart. You can decide to give away some small bracelets to people before you ask for a donation. This can make the other people you encounter feel indebted since they have received the bracelet, and they are more likely to help you out.
- After you helped someone move some of their items out of an apartment, you could ask them to help you move in a few weeks, or help you with watching your dog when you are out of town. They are more likely to agree because you already helped them out.

Common Manipulation Techniques

When it comes to persuasion, you spent some time trying to convince someone to behave in a manner that you liked. It benefited you, but it also had some benefits for the other person. With manipulation, though, you are not as worried about the benefits that come to the other person. Sometimes the other person will be benefited by what happens, but your main priority is making sure that you will benefit.

As you are working with your emotional intelligence, it is important to realize that most manipulation techniques are not that great. Yes, they still require that you get to know the other person and be able to read them. If you can't do this, then it is impossible to be a good manipulator. But since manipulation is not going to benefit the other person, it is usually frowned upon when you are working on your emotional intelligence.

There are many different techniques that you can rely on when it comes to manipulation. These will be slightly different than what you found with the persuasion techniques above, but they can still be very useful for a manipulator who is trying to get what they want. Some of the most common manipulation techniques to consider include:

- Lying: Manipulators often rely on the skill of lying when working with their target. They do this in order to confuse their victim or to falsely allay any fears that the target has. Lying can be either keeping something from the target, usually some information that the target will need to make an informed decision or outright not telling the truth even if asked directly.
- Not telling the whole story: This is when the manipulator is going to keep some key parts of the story to themselves. This allows the manipulator to keep their target at a disadvantage.
- Frequent mood swings: Manipulators know how to have complete control over their emotions and can make these emotions come out whenever it is

convenient. They may be happy at one moment and then flipping out mad in another. This is meant to keep the target off balance and makes the work for the manipulator so much easier.

- Spinning the truth: Spinning the truth is often used to hide some of the bad behaviors of the manipulator.
- Playing the victim: The manipulator may be able to turn things around to turn themselves into the victim. They do this to get some compassion and sympathy from their victim. Since most humans are drawn to helping out others when they are suffering, this can be an effective way to get the target to behave the way that the manipulator wants.
- Minimizing: This technique is when the manipulator will try to downplay their actions. They will say that they didn't mean to do something or will try to get you to feel that you are too sensitive. This

allows them to shift the blame to their target rather than taking it on themselves.

These are just some of the techniques that a manipulator may use to get what they want. As you can see, these techniques are not as innocent and nice as the options for persuasion. Often these techniques are going to force the victim to take actions that they don't really want to do, but they feel forced or cornered into doing against their will. As you work on your emotional intelligence levels, it is best to stay away from techniques that involve manipulation, because these only focus on you and not on the other person at all, and many of these techniques are actually a sign of low emotional intelligence.

Conclusion

Thank you for making it through to the end of *Emotional Intelligence Practical Guide 2.0*. Let's hope it has been informative and able to provide you with all of the tools you need to achieve your goals whatever they may be.

The next step is to take the procedures that were discussed in this guidebook and use them to help build up your own emotional intelligence. There are many benefits to having a high emotional intelligence, but most of us worry that we will fall short in this area. With the tips and suggestions in this guidebook, it is possible to increase your EQ and see the great results in no time.

It doesn't matter how long it takes to get through the steps. You can work on one at a time, or try to implement them all together. Each person is different, and your starting point is different than everyone else's. The fact that you took the first steps towards understanding your emotional intelligence and giving it your best means that you will see success. Take that motivation and the steps in this guidebook to help you increase your emotional intelligence today!

Finally, if you have found this book useful in any way, a review on Amazon is always appreciated!

www.ingramcontent.com/pod-product-compliance
Lightning Source LLC
Chambersburg PA
CBHW030114100526
44591CB00009B/402